ZOOM IN!

Visual illusions and guessing games

An Hachette UK Company
www.hachette.co.uk

First published in the USA in 2014 by Ticktock,
an imprint of Octopus Publishing Group Ltd
Endeavour House
189 Shaftesbury Avenue
London
WC2H 8JY
www.octopusbooks.co.uk
www.octopusbooksusa.com
www.ticktockbooks.com

Distributed in the US by
Hachette Book Group USA
237 Park Avenue
New York, NY 10017, USA

Distributed in Canada by
Canadian Manda Group
165 Dufferin Street
Toronto, Ontario, Canada M6K 3H6

ISBN 978 1 78325 162 9

Printed and bound in China

1 3 5 7 9 10 8 6 4 2

Commissioning Editor: Anna Bowles
Publisher: Samantha Sweeney
Senior Production Manager: Peter Hunt
Production Controller: Sarah-Jayne Johnson

Picture credits:

Every effort has been made to trace the copyright holders, and we apologize in advance for any unintentional omissions. We would be pleased to insert the appropriate acknowledgment in any subsequent edition of this publication.

Magnifying glass - Shutterstock.com/musicman, 1, 4br, 15 Shutterstock.com/mycteria, 1b, 41b Shutterstock.com/Eric Isselee, 2-3, 10 Shutterstock.com/argus, 3t, 5bl Shutterstock.com/Marty Pitcairn, endpapers, 3bl, 11 Shutterstock.com/bubu45, 3br, 5br, 13, 47 Shutterstock.com/aquariagirl1970, 4, 8, 18, 32 Shutterstock.com/Apostrophe, 4cl, 29t Shutterstock.com/Marc Parsons, 4cr Shutterstock.com/Subbotina Anna, 4bl, 39 Shutterstock.com/Venus Angel, 5tc, 45 Shutterstock.com/Gurgen Bakhshetsyan, 5tl, 6b Shutterstock.com/Tomatito, 5tr, 31 Shutterstock.com/Mazzzur, 5cl, 17tr Shutterstock.com/Borja Andreu, 6t Shutterstock.com/Michal Ninger, 7 Shutterstock.com/Tumanyan, 7t Shutterstock.com/Kletr, 7b Shutterstock.com/Joao Pedro Silva, 8t Shutterstock.com/Tatiana Makotra, 8b Shutterstock.com/Rolf E. Staerk, 9 Shutterstock.com/Marc Parsons, 10c Shutterstock.com/StevenRussellSmithPhotos, 12c Shutterstock.com/Viktar Malyshchyts, 14 Shutterstock.com/apiguide, 16 Shutterstock.com/Norph, 16c Shutterstock.com/Igor Kovalchuk, 17tl Shutterstock.com/Steven M. Ross, 17bl Shutterstock.com/Jim Barber, 17br Shutterstock.com/mygoodpix, 18tl Shutterstock.com/Dan Thornberg, 18tr Shutterstock.com/Aaron Amat, 18bl Shutterstock.com/DeanHarty, 18br Shutterstock.com/Robyn Mackenzie, 19 Shutterstock.com/Artography, 20 Shutterstock.com/Brian A Jackson, 21 Shutterstock.com/ZiZ7StockPhotos, 22c Shutterstock.com/kamnuan, 23 Shutterstock.com/Lizard, 24 Shutterstock.com/tiverylucky, 25 Shutterstock.com/Jomwaschara Komvorn, 26, 29, 36 Shutterstock.com/argus, 26b Shutterstock.com/PardoY, 27 Shutterstock.com/chaoss, 28 Shutterstock.com/Eric Isselee, 29b Shutterstock.com/Stefanie Mohr Photography, 30 Shutterstock.com/Andreev Alexey, 30t Shutterstock.com/Dan Kosmayer, 30b Shutterstock.com/vitor costa, 32c Shutterstock.com/Melica, 33 Shutterstock.com/gresei, 34 Shutterstock.com/andreasnikolas, 35 Shutterstock.com/zhuhe2343603, 36 Shutterstock.com/noppharat, 37 Shutterstock.com/MikeNG, 38 Shutterstock.com/Gordon Bell, 40 Shutterstock.com/Africa Studio, 41tl Shutterstock.com/Andaman, 41tr Shutterstock.com/optimarc, 42t Shutterstock.com/almondd, 42bl Shutterstock.com/Tom linster, 42br Shutterstock.com/Eric Isselee, 43 Shutterstock.com/Imageman, 44 Shutterstock.com/Maxim Petrichuk, 46 Shutterstock.com/Ian 2010, 48 Shutterstock.com/grafvision

ZOOM IN!

Visual Illusions and guessing games

Ticktock

Seeing is... Confusing!

Things can look bizarre when you see them very close up. Turn the pages to find out what these odd-looking objects are.

Eyes surprise

What curious creatures have peepers like these?

Answers at the bottom of page 8.

1
sparrow
hawk
owl

6

2
fly
grasshopper
spider

3
alligator
fly
fish

4
sheep
squid
fish

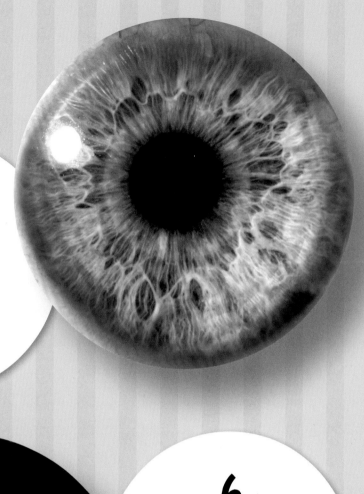

5

chimp

fish

human

8

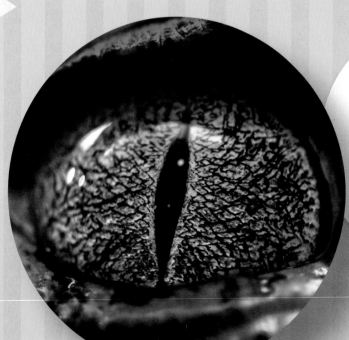

6

alligator

shark

chameleon

Soft and
silky-smooth!
But what is it?
Are those tiny stitches?
How do they glow
so brightly?

The biggest butterfly is the Queen Alexandra's birdwing, which can measure 12 in. across. It's the jumbo jet of the insect world!

It's a butterfly!

The amazing colors are created by tiny scales that scatter light. The effect is pretty to us, pretty to the butterfly's mate, and often scary to predators.

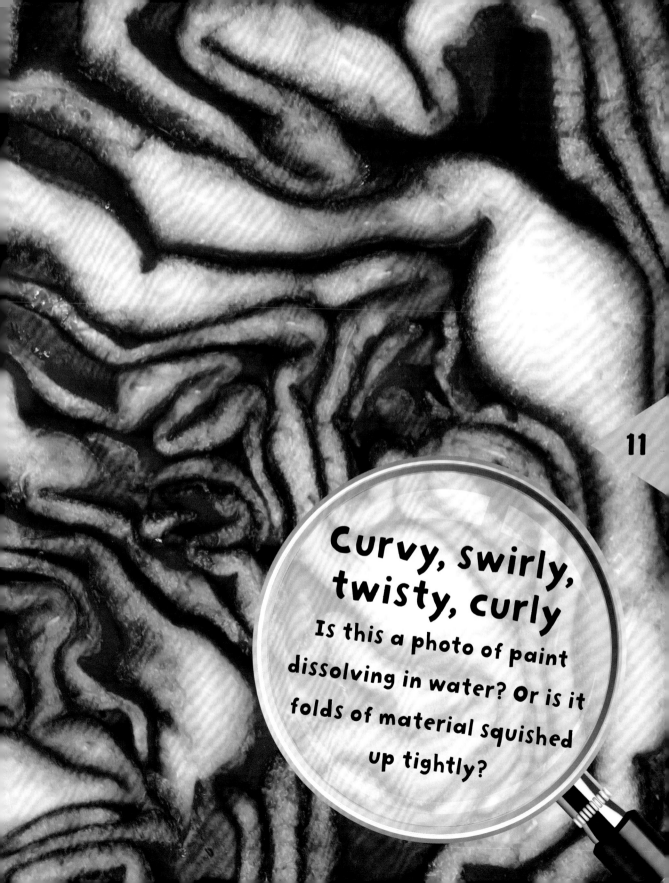

Curvy, swirly, twisty, curly

Is this a photo of paint dissolving in water? Or is it folds of material squished up tightly?

The largest cabbage meal ever was made in 2008 in Macedonia and consisted of 80,191 cabbage rolls. Yummy...

It's red cabbage!

The swirling patterns are made by tightly packed leaves. Cabbages grow by adding layer after layer of them until there are dozens, all squashed together.

13

It's grass growing on a rainbow!

OK, that's not true. But what is it, then? A tapestry? A woven basket?

A peacock's tail feathers can measure about 5 ft. long and each one ends in a colorful "eye" known as an ocellus.

It's a peacock!

Mr Fancy-Tail here is a male. He's spreading his feathers in a fan to impress females (peahens). They're gray, but they have an eye for colorful guys!

Tiny shinies

Is this some kind of plate armor? Broken CDs (they were really awful, OK)? Or a pineapple trying to be cool?

Some fish can have thousands of scales. Even huge fish like sharks have them. They're just too small for us to see.

16

It's a fish!

A fish's body is covered with small, shiny scales that overlap and produce a smooth surface. If you grab a live fish, it will slip right out of your hands.

Bulgy bobbles and furry fluff

They're all the same kind of object, though. Guess each one, then turn the page.

Football

Basketball

18

Tennis ball

Cricket ball

Obvious, if you just look...

This is quite clearly a bicycle wheel made out of pipe cleaners and a bit of sponge. Isn't it?

It's a dandelion!

Each of the little spinners is a seed, which whirls off through the air in search of a place to put down roots and grow a new plant.

Dandelion seeds can fly up to 5 miles away from the mother plant before finally settling down to grow.

Curled up, swirled up

Is this a view inside your body? Or is it the weird outside of someone else's?

The word "millipede" means "thousand feet." However, the most feet any millipede has is about 750.

It's a millipede!

A millipede has a body that is made up of hundreds of parts called segments. Have you ever held a millipede? It feels like being tickled!

Canyons seen from the air?

There probably is a place on Mars that looks like this!

23

Cork stoppers are made from tree bark. There's even a variety called (wait for it) the cork tree, which grows in Mediterranean countries.

It's a tree!

The outside of a tree trunk is covered in tough bark. It's like the tree's version of skin, and protects its insides from getting damaged.

Tree rings,
obviously!
But a tree was the previous
answer...

It's a tortoise!

A tortoise has a shell on its back. It can pull in its head and legs to protect itself from other animals that may want to eat it!

Tortoises can live for a very long time. Some have lived for more than 150 years!

This smells a lot!

Is it part of a leather saddle? A dirty old rag? A really stinky old shoe?

27

A dog's sense of smell can be more than a million times better than yours.

It's a dog's nose!

The tip of a dog's nose is usually wet. This helps it to sniff the air and work out where a smell is coming from.

Can you tell which fruit these pictures show?

Answers at the bottom of page 30.

1

pomegranate

cherries

redcurrants

2

plums

grapes

blueberries

3

grapes
apples
limes

4

apples
redcurrants
cherries

Answers: 1 pomegranate, 2 blueberries, 3 grapes, 4 cherries

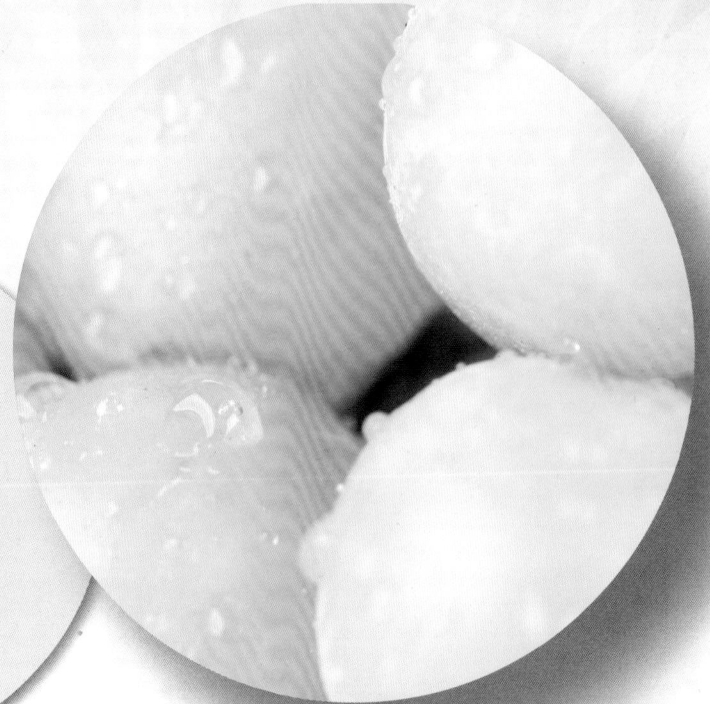

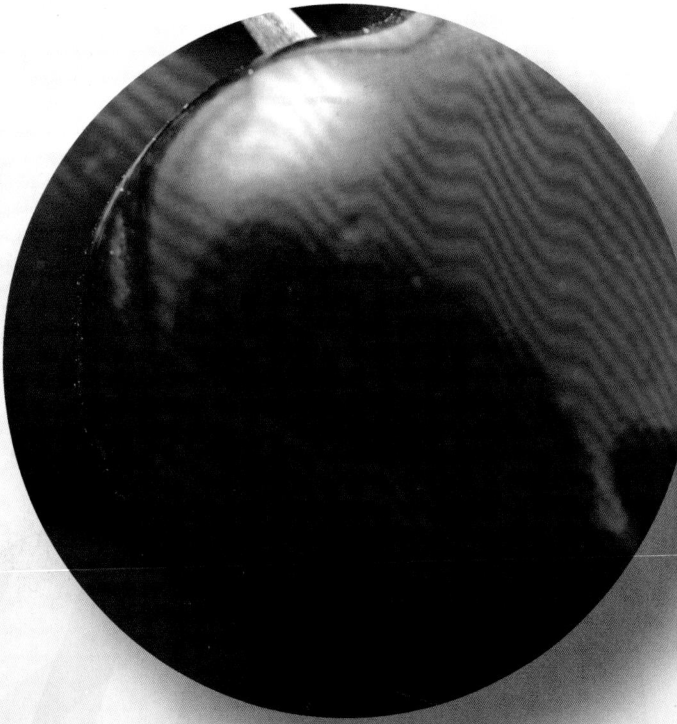

Stick 'em up!

This looks like the hair of a doll that is receiving an electric shock. But no plastic people were harmed in the making of this book...

31

Spaghetti gets its name from the Italian word meaning "thin string."

It's spaghetti!

Spaghetti is long, thin strings of pasta. It's also embarrassment on a plate if you have to eat it in public. Sauce in your hair, on the table, possibly up your nose...

Bumpy, lumpy, veiny...
Brain? Hopefully not, with that big gap down the middle.

It's a walnut kernel!

Until 140 years ago you'd have been jumping on walnuts to try to crack them. The nutcracker was invented in 1878, by Henry Quackenbush.

The biggest nut is the coco de mer. It measures up to 20 in. and can weigh 66 lb.

It's green!
(We just thought you might need a helpful hint.)

It's a leaf!

These huge leaves are from the banana plant. They're so sturdy and weatherproof that you can build one-story houses out of them.

Commercial bananas are all clones! The ones you see in the stores today are descended from a single fruit grown in China in the 1950s.

A whole lot of holes

Is it a bath sponge? Is it a bubble bath? Or something wholly different?

It's bread!

Bread is made of flour and water. If you add yeast too, the bread "rises"—bubbles of air appear inside it as it's baked. Light and fluffy!

Bread is one of the oldest foods made by people. Evidence shows it was being produced more than 12,000 years ago.

What's this lot?
Grains of colored sugar?
A microscopic view
of germs having a
family reunion?

It's a carpet!

Carpets are made from threads of material woven together to make a soft surface. Some are pretty luxurious—in 2008 a silk rug sold for $4.5 million!

The idea that red carpets are only for important people is believed to go back to Ancient Greece, when purple and deep red were thought of as the colors of the gods.

Different coats for different folks

Who lives inside these skins? Turn the page to find out.

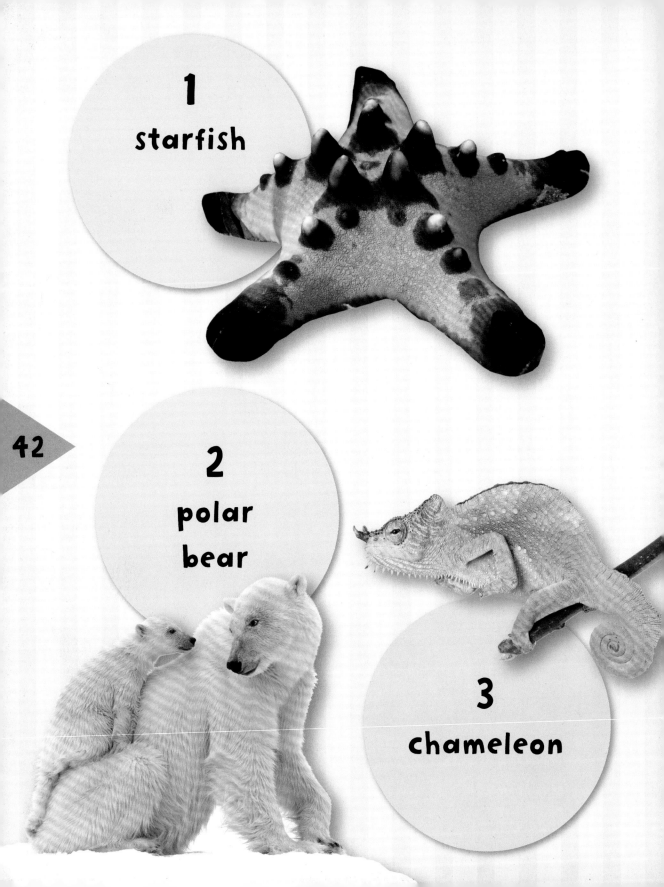

1
starfish

2
polar
bear

3
chameleon

Spiral stumper

Mmm, it's a bag of banana-flavored popcorn! Isn't it?

43

It's a sunflower!

Each sunflower can have up to 2,000 seeds in its head. They're often eaten as snacks, or turned into sunflower oil for cooking.

44

The tallest ever sunflower was grown in Germany and measured 27 ft. tall.

45

It's a bag of candies!

You don't believe it? All right, so you guessed correctly that this is a machine. But what kind, exactly?

The first watches were made more than 500 years ago.

46

It's a watch!

Watches contain a lot of tiny, precise cogs that make the hands move at exactly the right speed.

Could it be an
undersea forest?
Maybe this is what coral
looks like to tiny fish.

Romanesco florets are fractal, meaning each bud in the spiral is made of a series of smaller buds. (In other words, they're your math homework come to life!)

It's a cauliflower!

This variety is called Romanesco. It's a genetic cross between cauliflower and broccoli and it tastes nutty. As you might expect!